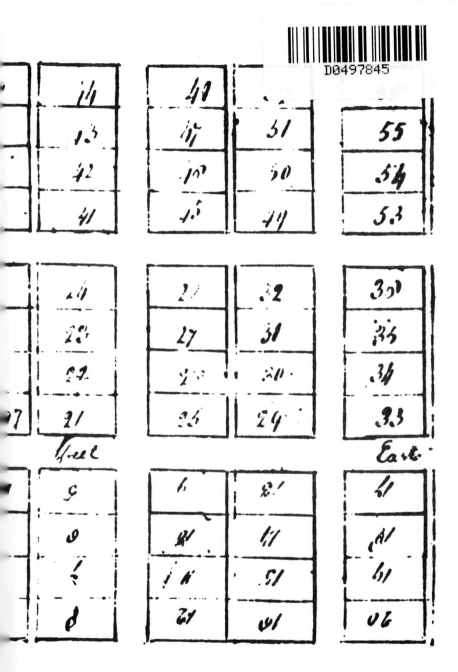

The Golden Lamb

by

Hazel Spencer Phillips

First Printing, February, 1958
Second Printing, June, 1958
Third Printing, January, 1961
Fourth Printing, April, 1964
Fifth Printing, September, 1965
Sixth Printing, July, 1967
Seventh Printing, November, 1968

Library of Congress Card Number 58-22478

CONTENTS

ILLUSTRATIONS

Photographs and Reproductions by Harold E. Rueppel

Foreword

Tavern keeping was the first business in Lebanon, there being a log tavern in the place when the town was platted in 1802.

At that time the tavern keeper's day began long before daybreak. Fires had to be tended, animals fed and watered, horses groomed and food prepared for departing guests.

Breakfast was a hearty meal of meat and potatoes, corn-pone baked in a dutch oven or jonny-cake baked on an ash board before the fire, honey or apple butter and hot tea or coffee. Dinner might have been roast beef or venison, leg of mutton, ham or a fat fowl, cabbage, green corn, turnips and potatoes with strawberries and cream for dessert. For supper: veal, cheese, eggs and ham, followed by pie, the classic American dessert made in large pans, according to tradition.

Rows of shining apples or freshly scrubbed sweet potatoes baked slowly on hot stones for the evening meal. A large mug of cider waited for the thrust of a hot poker to free its spicy, aromatic fragrance and send it through the inn.

With a good dry cellar under the house and a never-failing well of pure water at the door, the hard-working tavern keeper and his wife led their community in establishing a reputation for unflagging hospitality.

The tavern keeper's role has scarcely altered in the last century. The problems of maintaining an inn still challenge his ingenuity each day. Menus require the same diligent and inspired attention. Does the innkeeper's day begin later? Perhaps, but it finishes later and the arduous work never ends.

Little time is left for writing the history of an inn; and thus it falls to the historian to piece together the tale from public records, diaries, newspapers, letters.

Here is The Golden Lamb, born in 1803 with the new State of Ohio, an inn which for more than one hundred and fifty years has extended to the American traveler the warm hand of welcome.

H. S. P.

The Golden Lamb—Ohio's Oldest Hotel.

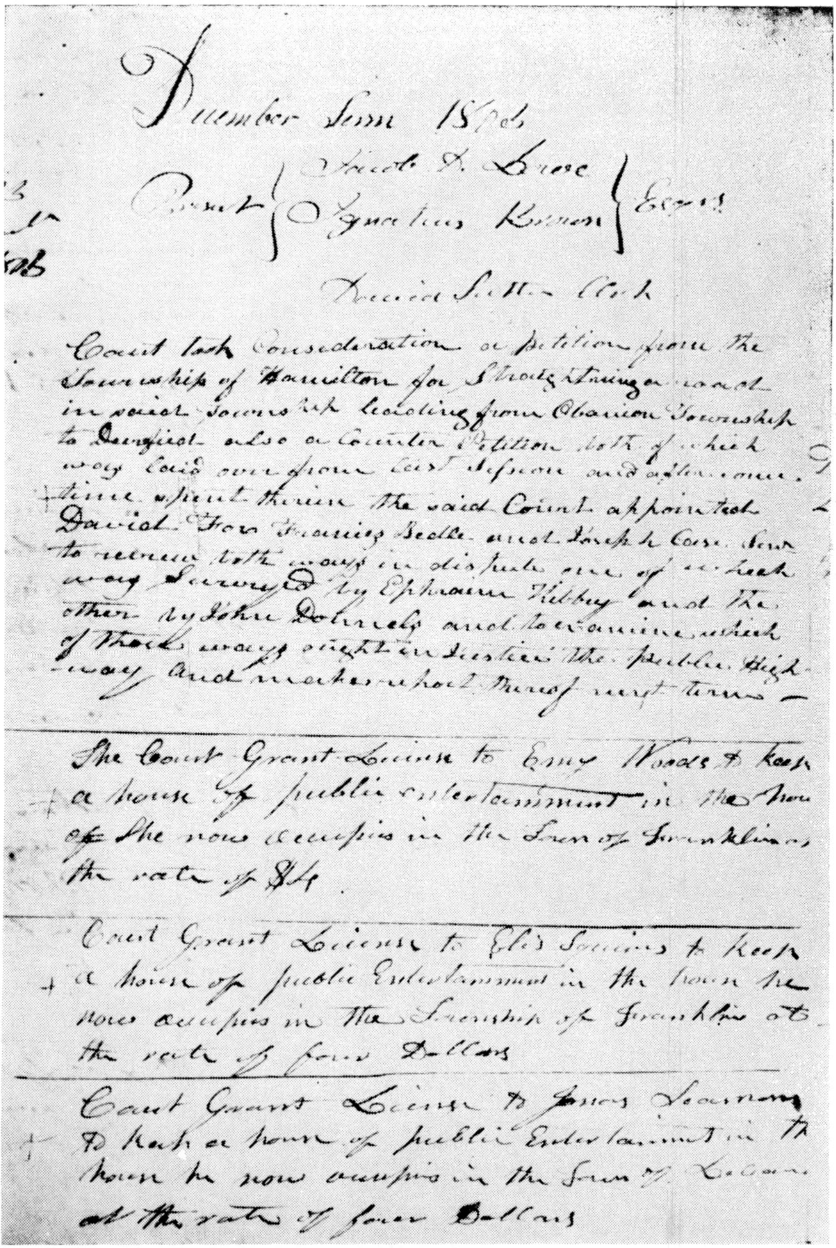

December Term 1803

Present { Jacob D. Lowe / Ignatius Brown } Esqrs

David Sutton Clerk

Court took Consideration a petition from the Township of Hamilton for Straightening a road in said Township leading from Clearcreek Township to Deerfield also a Counter Petition both of which was laid over from last session and after some time spent therein the said Court appointed David Fox Francis Beedle and Joseph Cone Senr to review both ways in dispute one of which was Surveyed by Ephraim Kibbey and the other by John Dobrrely and to examine which of those ways ought in Justice [illegible] the public High-way and make report thereof next term —

The Court Grant License to Emy Woods to keep a house of public entertainment in the house of She now occupies in the Town of Franklin at the rate of $4.

Court Grant License to Eli Sommins to keep a house of public Entertainment in the house he now occupies in the Township of Franklin at the rate of four Dollars

Court Grant License to Jonas Seaman to keep a house of public Entertainment in the house he now occupies in the Town of Lebanon at the rate of four Dollars

License issued to Jonas Seaman, December 23, 1803.

Original Deed to Lots No. 58 and 59 in Lebanon, Ohio

The Log Tavern

Our nation was a young land and our state, first-born of its union and confederation, an infant of less than a year when The Golden Lamb opened its doors to serve its first guests.

Two days before Christmas in 1803, Jonas Seaman appeared before the December term of the Warren County Court to secure a license "to keep a house of Public Entertainment" in the building which he then occupied in the town of Lebanon. David Sutton, who was then Clerk of Court and a tavern keeper in near-by Deerfield, introduced Seaman to the judges, Jacob D. Lowe and Ignatius Brown. The license was issued; and Seaman paid his four dollar fee. He walked down Lebanon's wide main street from the Black·Horse Tavern, where court sessions were then held, to his own new log house where his wife Martha waited for him. As his sturdy handmade boots crunched through the thin crust of ice in the muddy street, he mused on his future as a tavern keeper, but little dreamed of the long adventure, the events both sad and comic, that would unfold under the Sign of The Golden Lamb.

Jonas Seaman was born in New Jersey where his father William Seaman kept a tavern at Hopewell. Jonas married

Martha Forbes and came to Ohio with others of his family. Dr. Daniel Drake, in the Draper Manuscripts, lists him as owner of a lot in Losantiville in 1790. Anthony Howard Dunlavy names him as pioneer settler west of Lebanon in 1798. His sister Mary married Abner Hunt and settled near Red Lion. His brother Joseph settled east of town. Jonas Seaman brought his wife and children to Lebanon in 1803.

Seaman built a sturdy two-story log building on the lots he had bought from Ichabod Corwin that year. It was on a splendid location in the very center of the newly platted village of Lebanon, on Broadway, at the crossroads of the traveled paths of the north-south and east-west traffic.

Martha Seaman was a good cook, a thrifty housewife and an industrious woman. With a few servants to help with the weaving and spinning, the churning and soapmaking, the washing and ironing, she and her family set a good table and made up comfortable beds in clean rooms. The new and shining tavern soon became known as a fine place to stop for meals or a night. Its stables opened on Main Street and there were vegetable gardens, pig-pens and chicken-houses, a well, and other necessary houses, behind the tavern.

In 1805, when the first court house in Lebanon was built directly across the street, The Golden Lamb became more popular than before. It became the rendezvous for men of law and politics.

By 1807, when John McLean printed the first issue of *The Western Star*, other business men were already calling attention to their location near Seaman's tavern:

"Notice: The subscriber respectfully informs his friends, and the public in general that he carries on the cabinet making business, on Main Street, *near* Mr. Seamans tavern; where all who will favor him with their custom, shall be suited in the best workmanlike manner, and on the most reasonable terms.

February 13, 1807   George Miller."

Guests were served familiar pioneer food and drinks: deer, bear and wild turkey, hot corn bread and old fashioned apple butter. At first everyone was seated at a common table set with pewter, wooden and pottery dishes, but more tables were added as trade flourished, and Jonas Seaman soon had six tables set with knives and forks, glass and Queensware.

Good hot food and the inviting warmth of the great wood fires on open hearths encouraged travelers to linger at The Golden Lamb. Relaxed and well-fed, Jonas Seaman's guests talked of political and spiritual problems with the same fervor that fired the patriots at Williamsburg's Raleigh Tavern and New York's Fraunces' Tavern. Like men everywhere, they recalled—not without boasting—their own experiences in the wilderness.

Much of the news of the world was exchanged in the public rooms of the tavern, which soon became a clearing house for messages and letters as well, addressed to settlers and travelers "In the Land of the Miamis" and even "In the Ohio Country." As men met here to discuss their needs and those of their new America, the tavern became more and more important as a gathering place.

In June of 1803 Jeremiah Morrow was elected as Ohio's first representative in Congress. He came to The Golden Lamb frequently. So, too, did Francis Dunlavy, the most prominent of the early pioneers of Lebanon, who was president judge of the first circuit courts in Ohio. Both had served in the territorial legislature and in the long evenings of the early 1800's they talked over the days spent in Chillicothe, smoothing the political way for a new state. They discussed a letter, which had been drafted by Dunlavy and delivered by Thomas Worthington (later Governor of Ohio) to Thomas Jefferson. In it they had urged the removal of Arthur St. Clair as Territorial Governor since his veto obstructed every effort made toward statehood. Their experiences became familiar tales to the ambitious youngsters who crowded around and listened to every word.

Once a group of citizens gave a dinner at the inn for Jeremiah Morrow. They discussed a new road—an east-west road—to give access to the new states which were being formed from the Northwest Territory. Morrow was already familiar with the difficulties and hazards of travel on horseback. On his way to his first session in Congress, he, with two horses, had taken his wife and their two small children to her parents near Brownsville, Pennsylvania. He knew well the dangers of swollen streams, muddy trails through the woods. And in 1808 Representative Morrow, with Thomas Worthington of Ohio and Samuel Smith of Maryland in the Senate, introduced measures which led to the construction of the great highway from the Atlantic coast. This was known as the National Road, now United States Highway 40, which today extends from Atlantic City, New Jersey to San Francisco, California.

Early in March, 1805, farmers from west of Lebanon brought news to The Golden Lamb. Three men, they said, who called themselves Shaker missionaries, had walked a thousand miles from New Lebanon, New York, in the dead cold of winter, and were preaching at the old church at Bedle's Station four miles west of Lebanon. The stories of the Shaker's peculiar costume, their strange beliefs and their effect on the congregation amazed all who listened as guests gathered around The Golden Lamb hearth. The preacher Richard McNemar had with his eloquence persuaded most of his flock to renounce Presbyterianism and take up the queer habits of the Shaker cult. He was discussed most frequently. The converts were all well known to Golden Lamb habitues, who found it difficult to believe that prosperous, educated men would give all their worldly goods to this odd sect. Stranger still that they would renounce love and the family in favor of the celibate, communal life.

This was a tall tale if ever one was told! At The Golden Lamb eyes widened and whispers grew more persistent. It could hardly be true. Yet it was true. The Shaker commu-

4

nity, called Union Village, remained an important economic factor in Lebanon and Warren County for more than one hundred years. The Shakers' broad-brimmed hats and straw bonnets were familiar sights. Eager buyers throughout the country sought their fine farm stock, their medical herbs and concoctions, their furniture and other household essentials. Yet they never ceased to be an object of curiosity in the community.

At the turn of the nineteenth century, the problems of finance beset everyone. Debts and their collection concerned all business men, tavern keepers among them.

When Lebanon was platted the proprietors had not only offered sites for county buildings, but had agreed to donate the proceeds of the sale of every alternate lot for the erection of a court house and jail. In March, 1805, they delivered notes and money amounting to $1,241.80 to the county commissioners. With these was one for $100 given to Ichabod Corwin by Jonas Seaman in 1803 for lot No. 58. Court records show that Seaman, "on the 15th day of March in 1805, gave a new promissory note, in his own proper handwriting, for use of the county aforesaid whenever he should be afterwards requested." The new note was for $150. The additional $50 was added "for the use of part of the county lot back of the temporary jail on the Northwest corner of the public square."

In January, 1806, the commissioners, by their attorney Joshua Collett, brought suit against Seaman, among others, for failure to pay for their lots. A settlement was made but Seaman had to pay an additional $18.28½ by reason of the "Detention of that obligation."

Seaman, in turn, brought numerous suits to recover monies due him. One of these filed against Levi Estill in 1807, listed "$49 for one horse, also $150 due for meat, drink, lodging and other necessaries" furnished by Seaman. A partial recovery of this amount was made by Jacob Burnet, Seaman's attorney at that time. Rarely was he able to recover the full amount of the debt, usually settling for a very small part.

Jonas successfully defended himself against a claim that he was selling liquor without a license in 1809, but he was not so fortunate in solving his financial troubles.

The rising cost of living in the era is typified by the increased cost of the tavern license, for which Seaman paid $4.00 in 1803 and $10.00 in 1805. In May 1807 he advertised in *The Western Star* that those who owed him must pay their obligations immediately. His appeal met with little success however, and although his tavern continued to be a busy place, he was obliged to give a mortgage and finally in 1809 held a public sale to meet his own debts.

During the War of 1812, Lebanon became a meeting place for troops raised from the Counties of Hamilton, Butler, Clermont and Warren. Four companies of riflemen, one of artillery and one of light infantry were assembled in August, 1812 alone. Again and again notices appeared in the newspaper directing men's attention to meetings:

"Attention: The commanding officers of 2nd Battalion, 1st Division Ohio Militia, are directed to meet at the house of Jonas Seaman in Lebanon, on Saturday, 10th of December next." Captain Matthias Corwin organized his company and David Sutton brought his men here. There was a high flair of excitement in the tavern, where many dinners for officers were held.

In spite of all these activities and apparent prosperity, the Seamans finally gave up their tavern, and local newspapers recorded the fact that "a remorseless creditor forced a sale."

There is no known record of the time when this tavern first became The Golden Lamb, but since it was the practice of those early keepers to hang out immediately a gayly painted sign to attract travelers, it is likely that the sign was hung almost as soon as the cabin was finished. Because only about half the people could read, these signs were largely pictorial, following the English and European custom, with animals frequently chosen for illustrations. There was nothing unusual in the choice of a golden lamb—and nothing to indicate that it would reach the mature age of more than a hundred and fifty years. An advertisement in the 1820's proclaimed "The Ohio and Pensylvania Hotel *at the Sign of The Golden Lamb*" thereby locating this tavern *on the old site*.

Henry D. Stout, newspaper publisher in Lebanon and Franklin among other places, spent his early youth in Lebanon. He wrote a series of memoirs which are a source of much information of that period. In one of these articles he wrote: "That year (1812) our earthly parent bid us good day and marched with Captain Kesling to defend our frontier from the ravages of a British foe and his allies, the North American Indians, but, like many others, he never returned to his family. The barracks were located near Silver Street and it was from here we witnessed the first corpse of a soldier buried in the old graveyard.

In Lebanon, recently, after a long absence, we were reminded of those incidents. But we felt like a stranger in a strange city. Nearly all the old landmarks, together with the men of that day, have disappeared. On Broadway the old sign of The Golden Lamb alone remained."

Jonas Seaman was a witness to the will of his brother-in-law, Aaron Hunt, in 1819, but no further record of his presence in Lebanon after that date has been located.

Ichabod Corwin, one of the founders of Lebanon, and original owner of the lots, bought the old Seaman house. He built a fine brick hostel to replace the old log tavern and thus began a new chapter in the history of The Golden Lamb.

Black Horse Tavern where first courts in County were held.

Ephraim Hathaway's tavern sign.

Ohio and Pennsylvania
HOTEL.

SIGN OF THE

GOLDEN LAMB.

THE subscriber respectfully tenders his thanks for the liberal enconragement he has already received, and has the pleasure of informing the public that he has made very handsome improvements to the Hotel, which are now complete, and not excelled by many in the west, where Ladies and Gentlemen who may think proper to favor him with call, will find good accommodation; he will endeavor by diligent attention to provide his table with the best the country affords, and his bar with the choiest liquors; his stable shall also be well furnished with all necessary provender and a careful and attentive hostler.

By the publics humble serv't.

HENRY SHARE.

Lebanon, April 10, 1827.

Advertisement of Henry Share from *The Western Star.*

Stage Coach Days

Ichabod Corwin was an expert at tavern building. In 1798 he had built the log cabin which Ephraim Hathaway bought and operated as The Black Horse, Lebanon's first tavern. In this same inn the first county courts were held, and from it Jonas Seaman obtained his own license in 1803. Because such illustrious visitors as Bishop Asbury praised the stability of this community, Corwin felt secure with his handsome new brick tavern.

The early taverns had bells which were used to call guests to meals. Morris Birkbeck, an English traveler who came to Lebanon on June 22, 1817, wrote that before they entered the town they heard "the supper bells of the tavern and arrived just in time to take seats at the table, among just such a set as I would have expected to meet at the ordinary in Richmond—travelers like ourselves, with a number of store-keepers, lawyers and Doctors, men who board at the tavern and make up a standing company for the public table."

Ephraim Hathaway, A. Hill and several others operated the new tavern for short periods, until finally this advertisement appeared in *The Western Star*:

"Private Entertainment. The subscriber respectfully informs his friends and the public generally that he has opened a House of Public Entertainment in that new and commodious brick building on Broadway, adjoining the public ground, and nearly opposite the Court House, where those who may favor him with any call may rest assured of being accommodated in the best manner.

February 25, 1818   Benjamin Rue."

Benjamin Rue, a Captain in the American Revolution, had come to the Ohio country to build a fieldstone tavern at the ford on the Little Miami River, near the prehistoric earthworks now called Fort Ancient. Early in 1818 he and his wife rented their tavern and came to Lebanon to manage Corwin's place. Later in the year the following advertisement in the same paper indicated that he had been successful:

"Great Bargain—valuable farm and tavern stand, 6 miles east of Lebanon, where the state road from Cincinnati to Chillicothe crosses the Little Miami River.

Benjamin Rue."

Rue was a colorful figure and popular host. He continued to dress in small-clothes, the fashion of Revolutionary times and when he died was buried with full military honors.

Isaac Butler and his Pilgrims arrived in Lebanon on a cold February day in 1818. Fifty-five filthy, ragged, men, women and children in various kinds of conveyances stopped in front of The Golden Lamb.

It is recorded in *The Western Star* of that date that they were abject in following the Prophet's every command, and that "one mother, not quite destitute of feeling for her infant, thirsting and weeping, applied for some water for her child to drink. But Alas! The reply from the Prophet was, "If it cannot fast, let it die."

This band of fanatics received a cold welcome. The next day they proceeded to the Shaker Village and were given food and shelter—although the Shakers reported that their

10

friendly overtures were scarcely appreciated.

Isaac Butler, of Vermont, being miraculously cured of a severe back injury, believed the Lord had restored him to be a Prophet. He was commanded to collect his people and lead them to the promised land. Gathering his pious neighbors he held his cane upright and let it go and whichever way it fell that way they must go. Almost 100 people started toward the southwest with this self-appointed prophet. As they progressed on their journey frequent revelations came to him. His disciples practiced self-denial to mortify the flesh and became filthy in body and habits and gradually decreased in numbers.

After they left the Shaker Village they stopped at Mason and many were stricken and died of smallpox. The survivors wandered on.

Early in 1820 Mr. and Mrs. Henry Share came from Dauphine County, Pennsylvania, and became the proprietors of this already famous hotel and operated it very successfully together until the death of Mr. Share in 1830; then Mary Share stayed on alone for seven years.

The tavern had by this time become virtually a house of public entertainment. Early advertisements announce animals, acts, freaks and plays to amuse the people of the town and county.

The earliest entertainers were players who gave readings or acts. The advertisements in local papers grew from a few short lines to occupy full half pages, while the small handbills became huge placards in a few years.

Since Lebanon had no stage and few public buildings in which entertainments could be produced, the tavern became the town's first theatre. At The Golden Lamb a stage was constructed by William Wiles, a local cabinet maker, and the play was on.

In 1823, behind the scenes of the hastily constructed theatre in the hall of The Golden Lamb, Edwin Forrest looked over a proof of the program he had left in the office of *The Western Star*.

He anxiously awaited the arrival of his company and peered around the corner to Turtle Creek bridge on the road to Hamilton, until they came in sight. Because they were the first theatrical troop to visit Lebanon, many young boys and old men were greatly interested and lingered near The Golden Lamb. The doors opened at five, the entertainment began at six: admission was twenty-five cents.

At the first performance Forrest played Norvall. A Miss Riddle was leading lady and Jack Anderson was comedian. Thomas Corwin who attended, praised the young Forrest highly and predicted correctly that he would become one of the leading tragedians of the age.

The first two Saturday nights were a huge success, but on the third, after all the advertising was out, a young stranger died at the hotel. Out of respect for the dead, the performance was postponed. Forrest sat in his room and composed a poem in his memory.

The Western Star tells the story: "Mr. James Armstrong, Hatter, died after two weeks illness at Henry Share's Hotel. Dr. Ross attended him, an entire stranger, from Virginia.

August 16, 1823."

One or two more performances were given with small financial returns. The company's license, printing costs, board bills and rooms could not be paid. Their wardrobe and scenery were attached by creditors. Finally Cameron and Sellers of *The Western Star*, released them and took a note, which was eventually paid.

Old Ephraim Hathaway took them in his Jersey wagon to Dayton where they hoped to make some money. Forrest was seventeen years of age when he brought this troop to the Miami Valley. Years later he returned to Dayton as a great theatrical celebrity to open the famous Turner's Opera House.

Other shows came: a traveling museum, with upwards of one thousand curiosities such as birds, beasts, wax figures and an Egyptian mummy; good music on organs, cymbals and violins; then, most amazing of all, a grand natural curiosity, a large and learned elephant which walked from show to show, completely covered, and stayed one week in February of 1824. Many other attractions appeared until finally, on May 27 and 28, 1833, the world-famous Siamese Twins were shown in the Grand Room.

Patriotic holidays were celebrated with elaborate programs in those early days, when settlers still held fast in their minds the hard-won war for freedom.

On July 4th superb dinners were prepared by Jonas Seaman, Henry Share and others and served on the public square. These affairs frequently ended in brawls, and on July 4th, 1804, one of the guests attacked Jonas Seaman with his sword. Seaman brought charges against the man, Francis Lucas, who was a guest at his hotel. The charges read that "the guest Francis Lucas, with sword, staves and knives, force and arms, assaulted the said Jonas Seaman and did great damage against the peace of the State of Ohio." In the October term of court the jury decided that there was no way to collect damages but that "the defendent should go hence without delay."

There was always a parade, and an orator for the day would be chosen from one of the array of brilliant young lawyers from the community: John McLean, his brother Nathaniel, George J. Smith, Thomas R. Ross, or one of the two favorite speakers Thomas Corwin or J. Milton Williams, each of whom spoke many times.

On the 4th of July, 1823, Nathaniel McLean said: "We witness every day the evidence of our independence in the workmanship of your hands. How many manufactories have recently been established and produce a sufficient supply of articles for home consumption, for which, a few years ago, we were indebted to an eastern market. Let your town be a witness on this subject."

"The anniversary of the victory at New Orleans in 1815 was celebrated in this town on Thursday last. A Federal sa-

13

lute was fired at sundown, and a supper afterwards given at Mr. Share's Inn, of which 20 to 25 citizens partook."

The Western Star, Jan. 17, 1820."

The parlors of The Golden Lamb saw the inception of plans for Ohio's canals, for good roads, for railroads and bridges. Political rallies and celebrations were frequent occurrences.

In 1822 honest old Jeremiah Morrow, the last and best of the governors of the pioneer race, was elected Governor of Ohio. A delegation was organized in the hotel to notify him of his election. Among these was the erratic cabinet maker, William Wiles.

Tradition reports that they found Morrow working in his mill pond, looking more like a wet rat than a gubernatorial nominee. Wiles was so distracted by the appearance of the governor-elect that he never did recite the speech he had rehearsed all the way from Lebanon.

The largest gathering of distinguished men came for a dinner in honor of De Witt Clinton in July, 1825. In addition to Clinton, Father of Canals and Governor of New York, other guests were General William Henry Harrison, statesman Henry Clay, Governor Ethan Allen Brown and Jeremiah Morrow.

Governor Morrow and other prominent persons had joined De Witt Clinton at Newark on July 4, 1825, when the first spade of dirt was dug for the canal system in Ohio. On July 21st a similar ceremony at Middletown marked the beginning of the Miami Canal.

Preliminary surveys had been made for a branch canal to connect with the Miami at Middletown, so the entire party came on to Lebanon. They stopped at the Shaker Village on the way to observe that curious sect in its daily life and the proposed site of the canal through their community.

A signal gun on the hill west of town was fired so that the visitors were met by a large body of citizens and escorted to The Golden Lamb. A dinner was prepared that night at The Indian Chief Tavern, where they were joined by Henry Clay and others.

Clay had been detained in Lebanon by the serious illness of his young daughter, Eliza, who died on August 11th and was buried here after her father had gone on to Washington. Henry Clay and his family were frequent visitors in Lebanon as they journeyed back and forth from their home in Lexington, Kentucky, to the new nation's capital.

Politics always seemed important to Lebanon citizens. In August, 1826, there was a notice of a "Jackson Meeting at Shares' Hotel."

In November 1827, there was a Mass Convention at the court house to nominate John Quincy Adams for reelection. Following it a dinner was held at the hotel for the principal speakers.

From *The Western Star,* July 4th, 1826:

"The anniversary of American Independence was celebrated in this place in a manner worthy of the illustrious occasion. At 11 o'clock, A.M., a large procession of citizens and strangers, accompanied by Capt. W. H. Hamilton's Company of Lafayette Guards was formed on the public square. The procession moved to the large brick Presbyterian Church in the eastern part of town where a national salute was fired at 12 o'clock. After the firing ceased a prayer was offered, the Declaration of Independence read and an oration delivered to a house crowded to overflowing; the ladies of the town who never fail upon a proper and suitable occasion to honor us with their presence, were pleased to contribute to the honors of the day.

"The oration being delivered the procession again formed and marched to Mr. Henry Share's Hotel, at the Sign of The Golden Lamb, where a large and highly respectable number of gentlemen sat down to a most excellent dinner prepared by Mr. Share. Too much praise cannot be bestowed on Mr. Share for the elegant preparations he made for the occasion."

15

In the files of *The Western Star* on July 29th, 1826, we find the following interesting item:

Funeral Ceremonies

"On Monday last, the 24th instant, being the day assigned by citizens of Lebanon and vicinity for paying a tribute of respect to the memory of our late ex-presidents, Jefferson and Adams.

"At an early hour the citizens of the county began to assemble. The imposing solemnity of the occasion mingled with feelings of astonishment arising from the unparalleled coincidence of their glorious deaths.

"Stores, offices and shops were closed. The American Flag was wreathed with melancholy emblems of mourning and was displayed at half mast during the whole of the day. About 12 o'clock his excellency Governor Morrow arrived in town and was conducted to Mr. Share's Hotel; shortly after which a large procession formed and marched to the Presbyterian Church where the pulpit was hung with mourning.

"An Address was delivered by A. H. Dunlavy."

A testimonial dinner was arranged for John McLean on June 13, 1827. At this time he was Postmaster General and came from Washington to visit after a few years absence. A committee of his old friends, Francis Dunlavy, Jeremiah Morrow and Thomas Corwin was appointed to make the arrangements.

To honor the home-town boy who had made good, an elaborate banquet was prepared by Henry Share. In later years when McLean became Associate Justice of the United States Supreme Court and would-be presidential candidate at the Chicago convention which nominated Lincoln, many dinners were held here for him.

McLean combined the manners and the graces of the old school of jurists with the learning of the new, and was well-liked and kindly remembered for his newspaper career as founder of *The Western Star*.

Many other distinguished visitors stayed at The Golden Lamb. Three of these, the Earl of Derby, then Lord Stanley, later Prime Minister of England, with Lord Denman and Lord Dennison, all members of the House of Lords, visited for one week in 1827. They went hunting while here and met and visited with Jacob Grigg, a distinguished English teacher who had a school in Lebanon at that time.

An obituary in *The Western Star* on June 27, 1829, records the tragic stay of Judge Charles R. Sherman. Sherman, the father of General William Tecumseh Sherman, died when this son was but nine years old and had yet to learn that "War is Hell."

"Died, at his lodgings, in this town, on Wednesday last at 5 p.m., the Honorable Charles R. Sherman, Judge of the Supreme Court of Ohio, in the 41st year of his age. The deceased arrived here the Wednesday preceding his death. On the next day he took his seat on the bench, but before court met in the afternoon was seized with a severe chill. Medical aid was instantly called in, and for the first three days with apparent success. On Sunday his fever assumed an obstinate character and so continued to its melancholy issue. His attending physician promptly informed him of his danger, but relying on a strong constitution, he could not think of giving information to his family until it was too late to reach them, at his residence in New Lancaster, before his decease. A son, quite a youth, living in Cincinnati, and a near connection from Dayton, only arrived here in time to be recognized. . . . He has left a wife and eleven children—the youngest of whom he has never seen, having been born since he left home to attend the Circuit of the Supreme Court.

"On Thursday evening his remains were committed to the silent tomb, attended by a large concourse of citizens."

The old tavern was put to many public uses. At least one auction sale was held on the premises:

"Administrators Sale. On Saturday the 15th of August next there will be exposed to public sale at Henry Share's tavern

17

in Lebanon, all the personal property belonging to the estate of Benjamin H. Bright, dec'd, consisting of a YOUNG HORSE; lease for 2 or 3 years on a house and lot on Broadway in Lebanon, now occupied by Mr. Abby; Trunks, Saddle, Bridle and Saddle Bags and various articles of clothing.

"Sale to commence at 1 o'clock P.M. when terms will be made known.

July 31, 1829   A. H. Dunlavy, Adm."

When Henry Share died in 1830 the administrators of his estate were Thomas Corwin and Anthony Howard Dunlavy. Mrs. Share's interests were in friendly hands since these two young men had taken part in a strange test at The Golden Lamb.

It was the custom in those days for a young man who had completed study with a practicing lawyer in an office to apply for admission to the bar. Thomas Corwin and A. H. Dunlavy had completed their work in the office of Judge Joshua Collette and had applied for admission to the bar at the May term of the Ohio Supreme Court in 1817. It was then the practice of the court to examine applicants themselves, though they frequently called upon members of the bar to take part in asking questions.

After an adjournment of the court the entire company came across the street to The Golden Lamb where a large gathering of ladies and gentlemen had come to witness the examination. The applicants, of outstanding reputation as law students, were subjected to a strenuous examination which they passed with triumph. Corwin went on to become one of the nation's leading statesmen.

In spite of the friendly interest of her husband's executors, Mrs. Share found it was necessary to have a sale to settle the estate. It was held on December 10 and 11, 1830.

Before that date, however, certain items of the estate had been set aside for the widow and for the maintenance of her family. The list of those reserved possessions, together with the report to the court of materials sold, offers a record of the furnishings in The Golden Lamb at that time: everything from fine silver spoons to a large black bull. In 1830 The Golden Lamb was well furnished, its guests well fed.

Other glimpses of tavern life shine through accounts presented to the administrators. The most revealing of these is the account of cabinet maker William Wiles, a colorful figure in early Lebanon.

Wiles' bill includes a great variety of items purchased prior to 1830. The first, dated January 9, 1827 was:

1 small coffin, lined	$ 5.00
Case for do	2.50

Other items in 1827 included:

1 fancy bedstead (single)	7.00
2 washboards at 50 cents	1.00
Stage whip	2.00
Salt Box	1.50

The next reminds us that the stage had to be prepared for many entertainments. It reads: "To amount assumed for Harper the Comedian who could not pay for putting up theatre at your house August 1828 .... $10.00."

The variety of services given by these early cabinet makers is exceedingly interesting:

1 3-tier Martin Box, painted	$ 6.00
1 lace frame, for daughter	1.50
New Gate frame	1.00
Mending Table	2.00
1 fancy bedstead	8.00
Quilting frame	4.00
1 Ladies cabinet (mahogany)	65.00
1 common bedstead	5.00

The total of this account was $206.68, a sizable amount for those days. Several of these running accounts evidently caused much of Wiles' financial difficulty, which was frequently aired in the local papers.

The complete inventory of the estate, which is included in the appendix to this book, indicates that The Golden Lamb of the 1820's was not only comfortable but elegant as well.

For many years after the court house was built on the corner of Broadway and Main Street, there was a lively rivalry between The Golden Lamb and a frame hotel directly behind the court house, on Main Street. This tavern was called The Indian Chief; William Ferguson was its proprietor.

These taverns contended for the stage coach stops and for many years neither was satisfied, for when the coaches from Sandusky to Cincinnati stopped at The Golden Lamb on Broadway, those from Lancaster to Cincinnati stopped at The Indian Chief on Main Street.

From the time of William Ferguson's death in 1831, The Golden Lamb was recognized as the first hotel in the town. As in the previous years, trades and professional men located their places of business by it.

"Dr. Dickey, having located himself in Lebanon, respectfully offers his services to the inhabitants. His office is on Broadway, 2 doors north of Mr. Nixons. Place of boarding, Golden Lamb Hotel.

July 12, 1832."

"James Hopkins—Book Binding in the town of Lebanon on Broadway Street, a few doors north of Mrs. Share's Hotel.

September 13, 1832."

"George Miller, Coppersmith and Tinning, on Broadway, nearly opposite Mr. Share's Tavern.

February 1826."

"Saddles, Bridles and Harness, 2 doors South of Mr. Henry Share's Tavern.

Henry Bretney

June 23, 1826   John Hooper."

A well known silversmith began advertising his own and his wife's shops as early as 1808 and continued for many years. An interesting example follows:

"Removed. I have removed my shop from the west side of Broadway to the East side, where the clock and watch making business will be carried on as usual. Silverware, steel and gilt watches, chains, seals, keys etc. on as reasonable terms as any in the state, a continuance of public patronage is solicited.

N. B. First rate drums for sale. Thomas Best

Miss Best, Adjoining said shop

SIGN OF THE GOLDEN BONNET

carries on the Silk, Leghorn and Straw business and hopes from her attention and execution of her work to merit a continuance of public patronage.

August 19, 1826."

Several other concerns carried the *Golden* idea in their shop names. One other was a drug store nearby at The Sign of The Golden Mortar.

By 1832, Mary Share's advertisements were more important:

"Sign of The Golden Lamb. Mrs. Share very respectfully presents her compliments to her old friends and the public in general, and says that she continues to keep a House of Public Entertainment, at the above stand on Broadway, Lebanon. She flatters herself that from additional exertions to accommodate all who may favor her with their custom, that her house will be inferior to none in the state. Her house is large and capacious, with a great number of rooms made clean and wholesome. Private families wishing to spend a few months in the place during the summer season can be accommodated.

The Western Star March 12, 1832."

Mary Share continued to operate The Golden Lamb for seven years after her husband's death, finally selling to John and Aaron Pauly, who kept it for only a short time.

The Golden Lamb continued to beckon famous people to enjoy its charm and hospitality.

The Western Star of Friday, June 21st, 1833, records the visit of that great orator, Daniel Webster: "Mr. Webster participated in a public dinner at Cincinnati on Wednesday last. He arrived here last evening and left this morning on his return to the east."

When William Henry Harrison spoke here early in the famous presidential campaign of 1840, the hotel seethed with campaign excitement. It was a big year for Lebanon. By happy coincidence Tom Corwin, the Wagon Boy of 1812, was a candidate for governor and the Commander of the Army a candidate for president.

Corwin began the first of the modern speech-making campaign tours. His speeches for William Henry Harrison brought his own career into political focus. Corwin was a persuasive orator, with the presence, the poise, the voice, and the unconscious gesture of the great speakers of history. He was an eloquent artist with words; and at the time of his election as governor, he was the most popular man in Ohio.

One of the biggest events in the taverns' early history was the elaborate dinner prepared to celebrate the arrival of the first canal boat on June 9, 1840. This was the *Commerce*, with Captain Porter in command. It came from Middletown, loaded with distinguished visitors, and landed at the new warehouse at the foot of Mulberry Street.

The *Commerce* was a freight boat with a small cabin accommodating half a dozen passengers. Two or three hundred citizens of Lebanon and vicinity were taken aboard and treated to a ride down the canal a few miles and back.

On Thursday morning Captain Porter left the basin for Cincinnati with some 200 barrels of flour and whiskey and three or four lady passengers. The local papers began at once to carry advertisements of merchandise brought by this and other canal boats.

Stage coaches rumbled through town almost daily. Some were driven with four galloping horses, some with six. Drivers were showmen, jealous of their reputations, eager to impress bystanders with their ability to manage the charging beasts.

There were three stage trips a week to Columbus and two each week to Lancaster. Of the enormous traffic and travel over the National Road, a large portion of that destined for Cincinnati passed through Lebanon. More travelers came from Sandusky on Lake Erie, following the short route and taking advantage of the good road from Cincinnati to Lebanon.

People took great interest in the stage lines. Some of the coaches were handsome affairs painted and decorated on the outside and lined inside with soft plush. The now-famous Quaker Artist Marcus Mote fed his growing family for several years by decorating stage coaches.

Six cents a mile was the usual charge for passengers. The coaches stopped about every ten miles to change horses; the travelers dined at taverns along the way.

On a raw day in April the great English novelist, Charles Dickens, arrived in such a coach, and took dinner at The Golden Lamb, which was then called The Bradley House.

Tradition relates that he was a little man, wearing a beaver hat and a brown frock coat, that he had a huge fuzzy scarf wrapped around his neck to ward off chill spring breezes. He alighted from the top of the stage immediately after its arrival.

Followed indoors by his wife, her maid and his secretary, he demanded a drink. Calvin Bradley informed him that this was a temperance hotel. Dickens recorded his dissatisfaction with the visit in his *American Notes:*

"We dine soon after with the boarders in the house, and have nothing to drink but tea and coffee. As they are both very bad, and the water is worse, I ask for brandy; but it is a temperance hotel, and spirits were not to be had for love or money. This preposterous forcing of unpleasant drinks down the reluctant throats of travelers is not uncommon in America, but I never discovered that the scruples of such wincing landlords induced them to preserve any unusually nice balance between the quality of their fare and their scale of charges; on the contrary I rather suspected them of diminishing the one and exalting the other, by way of recompence for the loss of their profit on the sale of spiritous liquors. After all, perhaps, the plainest course for persons of such tender

23

conscience would be a total abstinence from tavern keeping."

Newspaper clippings some time after the publication of his *American Notes* reveal other incidents related to this trip: As the coach drove up several men were sitting "within the colonade of the inn." One of these, sitting in a rocker, was Judge Kesling, Beau Brummel of the village, and a regular boarder at the hotel. Kesling was a well mannered man who was always particular about his high collar, stock and ruffled shirt. He wore his blue swallow tail coat with brass buttons. On that day he was 45 years old and could complacently look back on a career of political greatness—for he had been Sheriff, a Representative in the Legislature and an Associate Judge. He was proud of his military career and had been a Captain in the War of 1812. He had been editor of a Democratic Paper in Lebanon and Columbus.

Dickens, on the drivers box, observed: "as the coach stops, a gentleman in a straw hat looks out of the window and remarks "I reckon that's the Judge, isn't it?" The Judge—still rocking—"Yes, Sir." "Warm weather, Judge," "Yes, Sir." "I calculate you'll have got through that case of the corporation by this time?" "Yes, Sir." "How did the verdict go—Sir?" "For the defendant, Sir."

Further remarks: "This coach is rather behind time today, I guess," and the inevitable reply "Yes, sir, nigh upon two hours."

The Judge lived to enjoy his reputation for many years after this incident; he swore that he never had an honor equal to that of figuring as a character in the works of the great Dickens.

After dinner the famous author received the calls of a number of leading citizens, among whom was Judge George Kesling, then took the coach again on the way to Columbus.

Tradition also relates that after Dickens had asked for his drink which was not available, he walked down the street to the tavern of William Wiles where these two short tem-

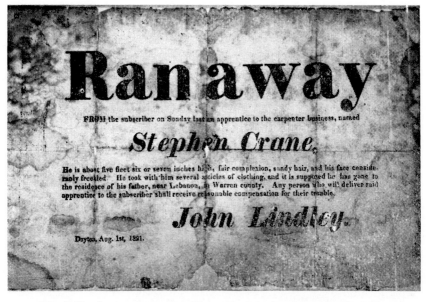

Handbill of runaway apprentice posted in local taverns in 1821.
(from Glendower Museum)

Lebanon in 1846. Henry Howe's *Historical Collection of Ohio.*

SIAMESE

THE TWINS.

FOR *Two* DAYS ONLY.

It is very respectfully made known to the Ladies and Gentlemen of *Lebanon* and its neighborhood, that an opportunity is now offered to such as have a desire to see the young men known as the

SIAMESE TWIN BROTHERS

who have excited so much astonishment wherever they have been seen, from the extraordinary manner in which their bodies are joined together. They will be at *Mrs. Shine's Hotel* on *Monday & Tuesday 27th & 28th May*

ADMITTANCE 25 CENTS.—The hours of admission to their room, will be from 2 until 4 o'clock in the afternoon, and from 7 until 9 in the evening.

☞ PAMPHLETS, containing an historical account, and also a full length portrait of the TWINS, can be had in their room *only*—price 25 cents.

Printed at the Journal and Focus Office, Louisville, Ky.

Handbill of Siamese Twins in 1833.

(from Glendower Museum)

pered gentlemen clashed in an argument.

These incidents could be true. Judge Kesling was a regular boarder at the tavern for many years, and William Wiles did have a tavern, The Henry Clay House, a few doors south on Broadway. This tavern was operated in turn by Wm. M. Wiles, the eccentric cabinet maker; William Wiles and E. A. Wiles, who was the manager of The Golden Lamb at one time.

Dicken's visit was noted in the usual brief paragraph in *The Western Star* dated Friday, April 23, 1842: "Mr. Dickens and Lady passed through this place on Wednesday, on their way to Columbus and thence to the Lakes. Mr. D. has been traveling, for two weeks past, very quietly in the west, visiting Cincinnati, Louisville, and St. Louis, with intermediate towns; and we have been gratified to observe the total absence of all that parade and sycophancy which characterized his reception in the Eastern cities. It will give us a better opinion of ourselves if even Mr. Dickens should not think the better of us for it."

Calvin Bradley had leased the hotel in 1839. His card appeared in *The Western Star* in May of that year:

"Golden Lamb Hotel, Corner of Main Street and Broadway, Lebanon, Ohio. The subscriber has taken and fitted up this well known stand, and is now prepared to accommodate all who may favor him with a call. General Stage House for Cincinnati, Columbus and Wheeling. Also for Lancaster, Circleville, Hamilton and Dayton. Hacks Carriages, Horses and Coach furnished at a moments warning.

May 10, 1839   C. Bradley."

A later advertisement appearing in *The Cincinnati Gazette* and *The Ohio State Journal*, as well as the local papers, would indicate some difficulty with this arrangement.

"A RARE CHANCE. GOLDEN LAMB HOTEL FOR SALE. The house is large and commodious. The stabling sheds etc. are large and convenient. Perhaps there is no place west of the mountains that presents as great inducements for a profitable investment. If not sold against the first of February it will be for rent.

November 13, 1839

December 27, 1839   John Hageman
                                            George Longstreth
                                             Simeon Sellers."

In February 1841 Isaac Stubbs bought the building for $3150.00. He sold it to Calvin Bradley one month later for $6700.00.

The new owner was a fine host. The memories of his splendid dinners prepared for visiting dignitaries were written of by state journalists for more than forty years after his death. His daughters married well. One became the wife of Judge Josiah Keck; another as the wife of Julius Botlan, became a noted hostess.

Accounts of celebrations mention the fine food prepared, the splendid banquets served, or the gracious hospitality of the hotel's genial host, Calvin Bradley, again and again.

The Anti-Masonic movement swept the nation about 1826 and continued many years. Masons were subjected to hindrances, abuses and indignities.

The Lebanon lodge was unable to secure a meeting place for several years. In 1842 a room was secured in The Golden Lamb, then being operated by Calvin Bradley, and the Masons were able to resume meetings under the old charter with the original Bible presented by Thomas R. Ross in 1815.

A most unusual advertisement in *The Western Star* on November 24, 1843, reveals some of the difficulties Bradley encountered as owner of The Golden Lamb:

"The Wreck

The well-built ship 'Bradley House', while running along the coast of uncertainty, encountered a dense fog, which gave great uneasiness to all concerned, as this was known to be a dangerous *coast*, upon which many gallant vessels had been lost.

"From the great efforts of the Captain and the perseverance of the crew, it is generally believed that the *Bradley House* would have cleared this coast, and made a safe harbor, had she not struck those fatal rocks, well known to mariners as the *Stubbs of St. Isaac.*

"After this effort to save the ship ceased, and the whole attention of the crew, as well as those on shore, was directed to the saving of the *Goods and Furniture*, which were scattered by the winds of adversity and were fast disappearing under the waves of trouble.

"A few of these have been collected, and will be offered for SALE on Saturday the 25th inst., at the "Wreck" for the benefit of the Captain and his creditors; among which may be found; 6 dining tables; 4 side do; 1 toilet do; 4 candle stands; 5 wash stands; 1 side board; 1 brass clock; 10 bed steads; 7 mattresses; 6 sets of chairs; 5 settees; 6 looking glasses; 24 pictures (framed); 1 side lamp; 3 spirit lamps; 6 sets of knives and forks; 4 celery stands; 1 doz. Champaign glasses; a lot of glass and Queensware; 1 Horse; 1 Cow; 20 Hogs; 1 two-horse sleigh; 2 men's saddles; bridles and martingales; 1 side saddle; 1 wheel barrow; 1 ice chest; 1 grubbing hoe; 1 spade; 2 iron wedges; 1 pair of large steelyards; and lots of other things.

Six months credit will be given.

Sale to commence at 10 o'clock A.M.

Calvin Bradley"

Calvin Bradley moved to Cincinnati and opened the Western Hotel on the southeast corner of Court and Walnut Streets in 1846. He continued to advertise in the Lebanon papers.

Isaac Stubbs repossessed the building and he and his heirs owned it until 1914.

The Stranger's Death

I saw the Stranger on his bed of death—
Sunk was his eye, and hard he drew his breath,
His quivering lips paleness had overcast,
And in dread agony his teeth clench'd fast.

Disease had now full skeleton'd his frame;
No soul did know him, or from whence he came:
A Stranger—friendless—in an unknown land,
His fev'rish limbs by stranger zephyrs fann'd.

Low on his matted couch, sleepless he lies;
No ear attends his deep convulsive cries:
'Twas night—the day had passed—no one did aid.
Or hover near where the sad stranger laid.

A deep fetch'd groan drew me to his bed,
And gently raising the sad stranger's head—
"Inform me," said I, "sufferer, of thy grief;
Thy woes in me may find thee some relief."

Ghastly he forc'd a smile—but answering wild—
"Oh! Heed me not, for I'm afflictios child:
In this dread state for two long days I've dwelt—
My cinder'd inwards have no moisture felt."

The stranger scarce his lamentation said,
When on the instant for relief I fled.
'Twas brought—and placed—ease to restore—
Too late, alas! the Stranger was no more.

I saw the body plac'd upon its bier,
And saw dropt on it one sad pitying tear
Bright gem of sympathy who gave it birth!
I thought such virtues were extinct on earth.

Upon the coffin now the clay was thrown,
Sounding mortality with candid tone.
A shriek was heard, and turning quickly round,
I saw near to the grave extended on the ground,
A *Maniac* howling requiem on the Stranger dead—
The only tear was that the *Maniac* shed.   E. F.

Poem written by Edwin Forrest at death of young stranger at The Golden Lamb August
1823. Published in *The Independent Press and Freedom's Advocate*, September 18, 1823.
—Courtesy Historical and Philosophical Society of Ohio, Cincinnati

The Lebanon House

The last half of the nineteenth century was a period of transition in politics, business methods and transportation, food and dress. During this era The Golden Lamb ended its stagecoach days and became a commercial hotel.

Isaac Stubbs, the hotel's owner, was a Quaker from Wrightsborough Meeting, in Georgia, where his parents and the ancestors of Robert H. Jones, the present owner of The Golden Lamb, lived on adjoining farms. He emigrated to Ohio with his parents and family in 1804. After learning the milling trade he built a mill on the Little Miami River. Around this mill grew a busy little settlement first called Millsbourough, later Stubbtown. When his business prospered, he built a good brick house nearby to live in. A versatile man, he engaged in many ventures, among which ownership of the Golden Lamb was one.

On March 7, 1845, Stubbs advertised in *The Western Star:* "That Valuable Tavern Stand, long known as The Golden Lamb Hotel, now The Lebanon House, in the town of Lebanon, Warren County, Ohio, is now for rent, or for sale. The House has lately been enlarged, and is in the first state of improvement. The Stabling, which is new, is large and commodious, and the whole premises well worth the notice of those who may wish to purchase or rent property of this kind.

29

A considerable amount of the furniture now used in the house can be purchased of the present occupant upon very reasonable terms. Those wishing to purchase or rent will examine for themselves. Possession can be had from the 1st to the 15th of April.

March 7, 1845.   Isaac Stubbs."

Several men tried their luck at managing it, but continuing advertisements signified that they won small success.

Samuel Egbert, who had managed other Lebanon hotels, had an advertisement on August 6, 1847, proclaiming himself manager of The Golden Lamb. E. A. Wiles, another tavern keeper, advertised it as The Lebanon House on October 29, 1847. Other managers were Abner Ross, C. D. Roosa, and Giles Longstreth.

It was evidently a good business, however, since new additions were made at frequent intervals throughout the years. One of these was a three-story wing made to the north of the original building by Isaac Stubbs in April, 1854. Years later, in 1878, the fourth story was added to accommodate the men who were building the railroad. A drawing made at that time, shows a full-sized wind mill on top of the hotel, indicating that some modern conveniences were available.

Whitlaw Reid, in his *Ohio in the War*, wrote that the village of Lebanon had been singularly prolific in its distinguished sons. This was equally true of its guests. Rutherford B. Hayes opened his first campaign for Governor of Ohio in Washington Hall, and was at that time handsomely entertained with a dinner at the hotel by local politicians. Presidents James A. Garfield and William McKinley visited several times when they were campaigning for office. President Benjamin Harrison was entertained here when he came to address a reunion of soldiers at the Warren County Fairgrounds.

Naturally, all guests were not so distinguished, and one at least, might be described as peculiar, if we are to believe an article in *The Democratic Citizen*, dated March 24, 1859, and signed Abner Ross.

"Story of stranger at Lebanon House. A Singular Circumstance. Last Saturday there came to The Lebanon House, a stranger, in a miserable condition—bare-footed, bare-headed, and crying in a pitiful manner. The family were greatly alarmed, as indeed were the whole neighborhood—and poor Mrs. ...... who you know is a timid woman, was so dreadfully affected at the manner of his coming, that she took to her bed, and did not get the better of it for several days.

Her husband, kind man, took compassion on him, and treated him more like a familiar than an enemy: and indeed if some one had not succored him, he must have died; for he was so weak, he could not possibly have reached the next town.

The neighbors were all willing as himself that the poor stranger should be harbored—they clothed him from top to toe. Generous treatment, you will say to one they had never before seen—and all the neighborhood admired it yet not one brought him an old hat or coat to put on. However, he was allowed to want for nothing.

You will naturally ask, who this person was?

Several persons talked to him, but not a word would he say as to his name, origin, object or country. Promises or threatenings have no effect upon him. His disposition is such that no ill language will move him. If you call him a rogue, or villain, he will laugh in your face. A discussion of politics or religion does not move him. As to his person, he is of engaging countenance, very fine eyes, he has no teeth, as though he was very old. But his having no teeth does not alter his speech, for he is as fluent without them as with them.

This extraordinary person is like a traveler that has been used to all sorts of company. He is never bashful, and is such a master of languages that if you speak to him in Hebrew, Greek, or Latin, he can answer you full as well as in English, which is his mother tongue."

Never a word thereafter tells us what happened to the man, who he was, or where he went.

31

In the 1860 census of Lebanon, A. S. Ross, Jr., is listed as the Hotel Keeper. Some of the guests living in The Golden Lamb at the time were: J. Milton Williams and J. D. Ward, Lawyers; Augustus Ward, Student; Houston Hopkins, County Treasurer; A. J. Roosa, Manager of Omnibus Line; Judson Morris, Printer; James Coffield, Tanner; Thomas Nisbett, Saddler; Phineas Colbert, Carpenter; J. W. Nipgen, Druggist; along with several Students-at-Law, a Book Seller, and others.

Board was from $2.50 to $5.00 per week, perhaps depending on the number of meals taken. By 1870 the cost of food had risen. The average cost was $4.00 to $6.00 per week, with about the same variety of professions listed as regular guests.

In *The Western Star* of April 25, 1861, there is news of the Civil War. The First Company of Volunteers to leave Warren County was Company A, Warren National Guards, with Rigdon Williams, Captain. The company numbered about 150 of the very best young men.

On Monday afternoon preceding their departure the Company formed at their headquarters, and preceeded by the Cornet Band, marched up Mulberry Street across Mechanic and down to the Public Square, where they raised an ash pole 75 ft. in height and ran up the Flag. There was immense enthusiasm when the Stars and Stripes unfolded themselves to the breeze.

Before this event a collection was taken up in the churches to place a Bible in the hands of each soldier, a fine flag had been presented to the Company and a sword to their Captain, Rigdon Williams.

On the morning of their departure, April 23, 1861, The Warren Guards took breakfast at The Lebanon House. The papers recorded that "Abner (Ross) gave them a splendid meal to start on, which the boys will long remember. Everything passed off pleasantly to all interested."

A few moments later, however, one of the army wagons ran over a small boy in front of the Hotel — and the paper commented "Mothers should keep small children indoors at such a time."

Many of these "very best young men" were leaving never to return, just as they had done in the War of 1812 and would be doing in all the wars thereafter.

In *The Western Star* of November 9, 1865, we read: "Change of Proprietors! The Lebanon House. The House is now open for the reception of guests, having been renovated, refitted and refurnished. The table is always furnished with the best the market affords, the cellar is stocked with the best wines and liquors, and the saloon supplied with the best cigars and tobacco.

We intend to make The Lebanon House a first-class hotel. No pains will be spared to promote the comfort and suit the convenience of guests.

Good stabling connected with the house. Omnibuses connect with all trains and The Little Miami Railroad. There is a daily line to Cincinnati, Mason, Sharon and Reading; and to Dayton via Ridgeville, Centerville; also to Franklin via Red Lion and Springboro.

November 9, 1863   J. W. Edwards and Co., Prop'rs."

In 1870, *The Western Star* announced:

"Lebanon House, W. H. Hart, Prop., Having secured a lease of this well known hotel for a term of years, it is now being repaired and put in good order," and a bit later: 'John Evans has assumed charge of *The Lebanon House* Wm. H. Hart, retiring. Mr. Evans informs us the house is for sale. November 10, 1870."

When it became apparent that an owner-manager was essential to profitable operation, Stubb's son, Albert, became the manager, to be associated with the hotel for thirty-six years. For a while he called it The Stubbs House, but the inn was more familiar to the traveling public as The Lebanon House, and the latter name persisted.

In 1871 Clement L. Vallandigham, one of America's most

controversial politicians, killed himself accidentally, in his room at The Golden Lamb.

Vallandigham is said to be the only Ohio man removed from his native state because of "treasonable utterances." The handsome young lawyer, son of a Presbyterian Minister, was the most notorious leader of Southern sympathizers, known as the Peace Democrats or Copperheads.

He was the most colorful figure in the hectic days preceding the Civil War. Arrested by order of General Burnside and tried by a military tribunal in Cincinnati, he was sentenced to "banishment beyond Union Lines." President Lincoln suspended in the case the privilege of the writ of habeas corpus, for the first time since the writing of the Constitution.

Vallandigham fled to Canada and became a Democratic candidate for Governor of Ohio. Although he polled a large vote, he was defeated for this office. He returned to this state soon after, resumed his law practice and became a popular public figure.

In June 1871, Vallandigham was counsel for a Butler County man who, charged with murder, had obtained a change of venue to Warren County. The lawyer's case hinged on the theory that the victim could have killed himself.

Demonstrating his plan to deliver the final address to the jury the next day, Vallandigham pulled his pistol from his trouser pocket. In a freak accident, the gun fired a bullet into his abdomen. Mortally wounded, he died the next morning. His client went free after a later trial.

Hotel arrivals were reported in the newspapers for a number of years. More than 120 guests were registered during the week of March 21st to 28th, 1881. They came from New York, Chicago and St. Louis. Others registered from Pennsylvania, Virginia, Kentucky, Delaware, Kansas and Indiana, and from numerous places in Ohio.

The arrival of the first train into Lebanon was a day of rejoicing and banqueting, for it crowned efforts of more than forty years and the expenditure of thousands of dollars.

LEBANON AND CINCINNATI COACH.

An establishment of this kind 'for the accomdation of the public, will commence running on Monday, the 1st of April, from LEBANON AND CINCINNATI, in the following manner:

Leave Lebanon every MONDAY, WEDNESDAY, and FRIDAY of each week, at 8 o'clock A. M. arrive in Cincinnati at 4 o'clock on the same days: and

Leave Cincinnati on TUESDAYS, THURSDAYS, and SATURDAYS at 9 o'clock A. M. and arrive in Lebanon at 4 o'clock P. M.

FARE—$1 25.

For seats apply in Lebanon, at the store of the subscriber, and in Cincinnati at Dennisen's Hotel.

This COACH is furnished with safe, substantial horses, and with an attentive, sober and honest driver, stopping at Sharonville for exchange of horses and refreshment.

☞ This line connects at Lebanon with the Dayton and Lancaster lines.

Leb. ap 2 83tf. WILLIAM SELLERS.

Stage Coach advertisement.

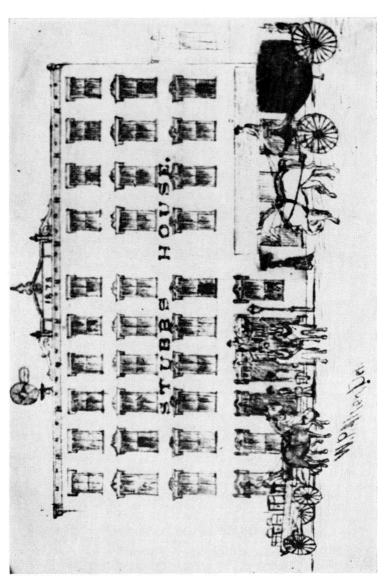

Stubbs House, from paperweight of Mrs. W. H. Stubbs.

The Lebanon House with Iron Balcony.

Guest Room at The Golden Lamb.

Dining Room at The Golden Lamb.

The first regular passenger train on the Cincinnati-Northern arrived on March 20, 1882, filled with the officers and directors of the railroad with more than thirty-five distinguished gentlemen from Cincinnati.

The train was met by over 2,000 Lebanon and Warren County citizens. A local committee including W. C. McClintock of *The Western Star*, C. W. Randall, J. B. Graham, R. H. Holbrook and J. W. Lingo, escorted the guests to The Lebanon House.

After a brief stop, the guests were driven over the city and shown the sights including the Corwin Home, the new Opera House, the National Normal University, the Reservoir and the many fine houses for which Lebanon is still today justly celebrated.

Returning to the Hotel, they were escorted to the spacious dining room decorated with evergreens and flowers, where an elaborate banquet was served. At the close of the banquet the excursionists re-embarked and returned to the city as they came. The citizens of Lebanon then indulged in a Grand Ball in honor of the day when the railroad came to town.

The menu for Thanksgiving, 1888, is typical of the services offered by hotels of this era and a far cry from the simple meals first served at The Golden Lamb. From *The Western Star:*

"The Lebanon House last week was in no way behind the hotels of larger pretentions in its Thanksgiving layout. Following is the Bill of Fare which Manager Pullin spread before his guests:

Blue Points
Cream of Chicken
Consomme Oysters
Baked White Fish
Potatoes Parisenne
Roast Young Turkey, Stuffed with Oysters
Cranberry Sauce
Roast Beef

35

Chicken Croquetts
Wild Duck, Currant Jelly
Broiled Quail on Toast
Celery and Lettuce, Plain or with Mayonnaise
Baked Mashed Potatoes in Form

Asparagus   Cauliflower
Sweet Potatoes
English Plum Pudding, Brandy Sauce

Mince Pie   Charlotte Russe
Vanilla Cream   Assorted Cakes
Fruits   Nuts and Raisins
Pineapple and De Brie Cheese
Coffee Demi-Tasse

December 6, 1888   *The Western Star.*"

Lebanon, keeping up with the world, was striving for culture. At one time there were almost as many students in The National Normal University as there were inhabitants in the town.

From 1878 to 1898 there were 309 plays, 71 concerts, 65 lectures, 31 minstrel performances, 19 operas and operettas, 13 readings, 5 prestidigitations and 58 unclassified exhibitions, a total of 571 public entertainments to which an admission was charged. This record was kept by Josiah Morrow.

The Golden Lamb, or Lebanon House, as it was then called, housed many of these performers.

With the coming of the railroad and the decline of stage coach travel, old roadside taverns were isolated and highways neglected.

As The Lebanon House, for more than half a century, this was just another hotel serving guests with indifferent attention.

The Golden Lamb

In the twentieth century the automobile brought good roads, the return of highway travel and the demand for suitable roadside accommodations and the slumbering taverns stirred to active life again.

In November of 1926, there came to Lebanon an energetic young man who had acquired both hotel training and experience in restaurant ownership during his college days at Antioch. It was Robert H. Jones, who is still the hotel's owner and host.

In June of 1928 Mr. Jones married Virginia Kunkle, of Springfield, and the following year their daughter Joan was born.

Mr. and Mrs. Jones launched an extensive remodeling program, providing maximum comfort with an early American atmosphere, compatible with tradition throughout the hotel.

The improvements included a picturesque colonial porch with tall graceful white pillars and second and third floor balconies.

The exterior was sand-blasted to restore the original appearance of the hand-made bricks, while the interior was completely furnished with antiques, some of which are original furnishings of the inn.

The building today has four floors, a lobby, four large public and four private dining rooms, a gift shop and forty guest rooms all with telephone, television, and air conditioning. The old stables have been removed to make a modern parking lot.

Mr. Jones has a rare collection of Shaker materials including documents, literature and furniture; an important group of Currier and Ives prints and an extensive collection of miniature lambs which have been sent to him from all over the world. These interesting and varied materials are integrated with the hotel furnishings to add interest to the interior.

The building and organization has frequently been singled out for distinction. The Golden Lamb was chosen as one of the buildings worthy of preservation in the Historic Buildings Survey and complete plans of the building are filed in the Department of the Interior in Washington.

In 1940 it was marked by the Daughters of the American Revolution as the oldest hotel in Ohio. This ceremony attracted thousands of guests among whom were Governor John Bricker, Former Governor Myers Y. Cooper and C. Bascom Slemp, who served as Secretary to Calvin Coolidge.

An editorial in *The Western Star* the following week paid a fine tribute to "Bob and Ginny" as they are lovingly called by Lebanon citizens: "The Golden Lamb was recreated, and through the ambition of its hosts and hostess, through private enterprise often unappreciated, Lebanon began again to be important. It became to many travelers and "diners out" a Mecca. Instead of being a place along the way, Lebanon and The Golden Lamb became the end and the purpose of the journey.

To Mine Host, Robert H. Jones and Mrs. Jones, Lebanon is deeply indebted and in acknowledging the obligation, Lebanon wishes for them the very best, knowing that their success will not be counted in earnings alone."

This marking had far-reaching results. In the May 2nd, 1940 issue of *The Western Star*, an editorial was headed: 'Should

Carry It Forward.' "It is time to crystallize the sentiment into an active working historical society whose function it would be to cooperate with the Daughters of the American Revolution and other patriotic organizations in restoring and retaining the old, the priceless relics of a glorious past, to the end that oncoming generations will better recognize the value of their heritage. Let us resolve not to let this opportunity pass."

The following week the Warren County Historical Society was organized at The Golden Lamb, and an active program to promote the knowledge of American history was launched culminating in the establishment of Glendower and the Warren County Museum.

In January 1956, the Turtle Creek Chapter Daughters of the American Revolution made their first presentation of an Award of Merit. This was given to Mr. Robert H. Jones "for his efforts and splendid achievements in the preservation and restoration of this historic structure, for his generosity to patriotic and educational organizations, for his active interest in Civic Projects, and for his Good Citizenship, essential in a Republic such as ours, all of which has been directed toward the preservation of the American way of life."

In 1957 Mr. Jones was selected for an honor bestowed by his fellow citizens. The Lebanon Chamber of Commerce presented their annual award to Mr. Jones as "The Outstanding Citizen Over a Period of Years."

The Golden Lamb itself has been the subject of many articles in state and national publications, including *Life, Ford, Gourmet, Duncan Hines* and *American Automobile Association* recognition.

Where guests once arrived by stage or on horseback, they now come in cars, buses and helicopters.

On foot, by horse or oxen-cart, in covered wagon or stagecoach, by canal boat or railroad car, by automobile or plane, guests have arrived to enjoy The Golden Lamb and its hospitality. They share the enthusiasm of *The Western Star* of July 11, 1957, which sums up the hotel's history in a single sentence: "The Golden Lamb makes for pleasant living and is the answer to a gourmet's prayer."

The Golden Lamb has retained its prestige for more than a century and a half. The colonial facade, on the busy thoroughfare which was once a stage route through what Charles Dickens described as a beautiful country, richly cultivated, presents an hospitable threshold for throngs of wayfarers.

Traditional furnishings, with modern conveniences, the tasty meals for which The Golden Lamb is known far and wide, combined with the friendliness of small-town hosts, give maximum comfort to the traveling public today.

In the lobby, as people gather around the open fireplace, strangers speak to strangers and the feeling of good comradeship persists. In the flickering candlelight one can almost feel the presence of all the good and great men of the past and hear the swish of crinoline skirts against the fine old furniture, hear the voice of Dickens echoing through the halls: "God rest you merry, gentlemen, let nothing you dismay."

With its legend of drama and romance that are a part of our traditions, The Golden Lamb is dedicated to the preservation of American Life and holds fast to a quality of gentle and gracious living.

Lobby of The Golden Lamb.

DAR Marker, Ohio's Oldest Hotel.

Daughters of the American Revolution

PRESENTS THIS

Award of Merit
to Robert H. Jones

In Grateful Acknowledgement and Sincere Appreciation of
Outstanding Services and Worthy Accomplishments for the
Protection of our Constitutional Republic.

DATED THIS *Seventh* DAY OF *January* 1956

Hazel D. Phillips
CHAIRMAN

Laura B Cunningham
REGENT

DAR Award of Merit.

Lebanon Chamber of Commerce

Citizen of the Year

1957 AWARD

This Certificate is Awarded to
Robert H. Jones

In recognition of his outstanding service to the community, combined with his interest in all things affect-
ing and bettering his Home, his State, and his Nation,
The Lebanon Chamber of Commerce gratefully presents this Certificate of Honor.

President

Dated this _____ day of _____

Chamber of Commerce Award.

·DEPARTMENT·OF·THE·INTERIOR·
·WASHINGTON·D·C·
·THIS·IS·TO·CERTIFY·THAT·THE·
·HISTORIC·BUILDING·
·KNOWN·AS·

The Golden Lamb Hotel

·IN·THE·COUNTY·OF·

Warren

·AND·THE·STATE·OF·

Ohio

·HAS·BEEN·SELECTED·BY·THE·
·ADVISORY·COMMITTEE·OF·THE·

·HISTORIC·AMERICAN·
·BUILDINGS·SURVEY·

·AS·POSSESSING·EXCEPTIONAL·
·HISTORIC·OR·ARCHITECTURAL·
·INTEREST·AND·AS·BEING·WORTHY·
·OF·MOST·CAREFUL·PRESERVATION·
·FOR·THE·BENEFIT·OF·FUTURE·
·GENERATIONS·AND·THAT·TO·THIS·
·END·A·RECORD·OF·ITS·PRESENT·
·APPEARANCE·AND·CONDITION·
·HAS·BEEN·MADE·AND·DEPOSITED·
·FOR·PERMANENT·REFERENCE·IN·THE·

·LIBRARY·OF·CONGRESS·

·ATTEST·

Charles R. Strong

·District·Officer·

Harold L. Ickes

·Secretary·of·the·Interior·

Department of the Interior Citation.

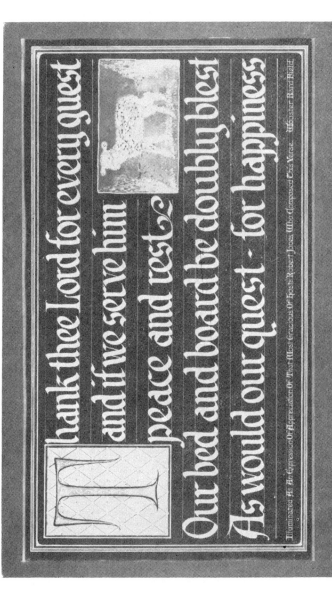

Peace and Rest, Motto by Robert H. Jones.

Conveyances

Village of Lebanon

Grantor	Grantee	Date
Corwin, Ichabod	Jonas Seaman	Aug. 19, 1805
Seaman, Jonas	Samuel McCray	Nov. 15, 1808
McCray, Samuel	Ephraim Hathaway et al	June 29, 1813
Hathaway, Ephraim	Ichabod Corwin	March 1, 1814
McCray, Rebecca	Ichabod Corwin	Dec. 21, 1814
Corwin, Ichabod	Mary Share	March 4, 1832
Share, Mary	Jno & Aaron Pauly	Jan. 2, 1837
Pauly, John et al	Geo. Longstreth, et al	June 21, 1837
Longstreth, Geo. et al	John Hageman	March, 1840
Hageman, John	Isaac Stubbs	Feb. 1, 1841
Stubbs, Isaac	Calvin Bradley	March 26, 1841
Bradley, Calvin	Isaac Stubbs	April 5, 1843
Iorns, Margaret heir of I. Stubbs	Albert & Isaac Stubbs	Nov. 22, 1880
Stubbs, et al W. H. Ad.	E. Stubbs, et al	Nov. 9, 1914
Stubbs, Isaac	S. S. Kilpatrick, et al	Nov. 28, 1914
Kilpatrick, S. S. et al	Ownly Furman	Dec. 2, 1914
Furman, Ownly	Ethel H. Furman	May 6, 1918
Furman, Ethel H.	Victor E. & R. Furman	Dec. 29, 1923
Furman, V. E. & R. O., by Gdn., Robt. H. Jones		
Furman, Ownly, V. E. & R. O.,	same	Aug. 2, 1927

Furnishings
of The Golden Lamb

The estate of Henry Share was appraised by W. Sellers, Wm. Lowrey and G. Kesling. The sale of goods and chattels was held on December 10 and 11, 1830. Before that date the following articles were set apart for the widow toward a year's maintenance. Appraiser's list:

7	Barr room chairs	2.50
6	Winsor chairs	2.00
1	large dining table (new)	3.00
1	set Madison tables	9.00
1	small breakfast table	2.00
1	mantle clock	12.00
1	pr. Shovel and Tongs	1.50
1	Bureau and Bookcase	8.00
1	Work Stand	1.50
1	ten-plate Stove and pipe	13.00
6	winsor chairs	1.50
1	large tea tray	.50
6	winsor chairs	4.50
1	wash stand, pitcher and bason	1.00
1	tea waiter and snuffers	.25
2	window curtains	.50
6	black winsor chairs	4.50

1	wash stand, pitcher and bowl	1.00
1	pr and irons shovel and tongs	1.00
1	single bedstead and bedding	5.00
1	bedstead and bedding (in garrett)	3.00
3	stable buckets	.75
1	reek of hay	22.50
1	barrell peach brandy (8 gal @ 62½	5.00
4	kegs	2.00
3	whiskey Barrells	1.50
1	large tea kettle	1.50
2	frying pans	1.50
2	grid irons	1.50
2	stew pots	1.00
1	griddle	.25
2	dutch ovens	1.25
2	ols benches on back porch	.25
½	doz Silver Spoons	10.00
1	soup turrean	1.00
10	glass tumblers	.75
3	sett plates	.75
1	lot cubbard wear in dining room	2.00
4	table spoons	.50
9	Silver tea spoons	2.25
1	caster and cruits	1.00
2	carving knives	.75
2	sett knives and forks	2.00
2	trays and 1 pr snuffers	.37½
1	carpet in the back room	5.50
10	table cloths	10.00
2	common qt Decanters	.50
2	ring pints.... do	.37½
2	qts........ do	1.00
5	mound quarts do	1.25
2	common gallon bottles	.50
1	half do do	.18½
4	common quart do	.50
2	half gallon jars	.75
4	Claret bottles and 2 porter bottles	.50
3	cruets	.50
4	kegs with faucets	5.00
2	blue pitchers and 2 enameled do	1.00
1	sugar box	.25
1	sconce reflector	.50

1	hostler bell		.75
1	dramer and 6 tumblers		1.00
6	iron candle sticks		.50
1	tin lantern		.50
1	barr tub		.50
1	lot slippers		2.00
1	lot Family books		15.00
1½	Barrell Flour		3.00
2	Meat Casks		2.00
1	tub with meat in it (Supposed to be 300 lb)		9.00
3	wash tubs		3.00
1	lot of barrels in celler		.50
½	barrel of flour		1.00
1	coffee mill, sauce pan etc.		.75
1	sive		.25
1	barrel Whiskey 32 gal @ 25		8.00
¼ do	do	8 gal	2.00
¼ do Peach Brandy			5.00
1	single bedstead and bedding		13.00
1	double	do	do	15.00
4	single	do	do	40.00
4	single	do	do	18.00
3	single	do	do	14.00
3	single	do	do	24.00
1	double	do	do	10.00
1	sett Liverpool Plates		1.25
1	sett Blue coffee cups and large dish		1.12½
1	lot china cups and saucers and knife box and knives		3.25

Total Amt. $360.81

Cash   39.18½

Total Allowance   400.00

The following list of property taken by widow at appraisement is attached:

Adams and Jefferson's last letters		1.00
1	set Britannia Ware	10.00
1	candlestick	.75
1	Dressing glass	.75
1	Circular Bureau	8.00
1	Stove in dining room	16.00
1	Womans saddle	3.50
1	large red Heifer	7.00
6	yellow chairs	2.80
6	red chairs	2.40
1	small trunk	1.00
2	Window Blinds	1.50
1	Bureau, columned	10.00
1	set andirons	1.00
2	stable forks	.75
2	pitch forks	.75
1	bush.and peck measure	.87½
1	old wheel barrow	.75

$68.12
Sale Bill 13.00

Total $81.12

The Bill of Sale of the Goods and Chattels of Henry Share was duly advertised for 20 days and sold at public auction. The list of articles sold, with purchasers, and amounts, as accepted by the court, completes the list of furnishings of The Golden Lamb at the death of Henry Share in 1830.

Mary Share, 1 stand		.25
do	1 stand and 5 benches	.93⅔
do	1 work stand	.50
do	1 rice carpeting	2.50
do	1 old settee	.81
do	1 old looking glass	.25
I. Corwin, 1 old stand		.55
Richard Skinner, 1 writing desk 9 bar room)		1.37
Mrs. Share, 1 candle stick, sconce		.06
E. Stowell, 1 sett Red Windsor Chairs		2.25
Mrs. Share, 1 looking glass		2.00
Thomas Serri, 1 Breakfast table		1.62½

Mrs. Share, 1 old dining table 25
G. H. Abbey, 2 small waiters 25
Jas Frasier, 2 pitchers 42
Thomas Smith, 1 Map of U. S. 5.37½
Wm. Sellers, Declaration of Independence and F. 2.57½
Wm. M. Wiles, I Masonic Chart 62½
Jas Frasier, Johnson's Sunday Mail report 51
Wyllys Pearson, Map of Ohio, small 31½
Mrs. Share, Chronological Chart 56½
Z. Stubbs, 1 Blue pitcher 44
Mrs. Share, 1 old waiter 12
Wm. Sellers, 1 large dish 50
Joseph Edwards, 1 broken sett Tea Cups & saucers 25
Thomas Smith, 1 pepper and salt celler 14
Mrs. Share, 2 old dishes 19
Jas Frasier, 1 china dish 07
I. Corwin, ½ doz plates 32
Mrs. Share, 1 looking glass 87
Mr. Taylor, 1 old   do 12½
T. Vanote, 1 old   do 56½
L. S. Ingersoll, 1 china dish 39
Mrs. Share, 2 rocking chairs 50
J. P. Halsey, English and German Dictionary 1.50
Thomas Smith, 2 vols Goldsmith Am. Nature 1.25
Mrs. Share, 1 breakfast table 2.75
        do   1 old server 06¼
        do   4 small candle servers .07
E. Share, System of Distillation 25
L. S. Ingersoll, 1 egg beater 13
Mrs. Share, 1 flat cake beater 13
                another 14½
Nich, Scott, Bottle 06½
S. Frasier, Bottle and pitcher 14
A. L. Ross, 2 sconce candlesticks 14½
A. F. Neal, 2 sconce candlesticks 17
Isaac Evans, large basket and lumber 33
L. S. Ingersoll, 1 set knives and forks 68½
John Lowe   do   .52
I. Hathaway   do   .32
I. Frasier   do   .62½
I. Corwin   do   .43¾
G. Rankins   do   .37½
B. Hathaway, 1 set small knives and forks 31½

I. Carter, Mattock and old tea kettle 18½
I. Corwin, Pair Harness 62½
I. Frasier, Small Grindstone 06¼
Jos Edwards, Iron tea kettle 43½
L. S. Ingersoll, Spade 35
E. Share, Steel Yards 25
I. Corwin, 1 old coverlid 18
S. Frasier, 1 jug 42¼
Wm. M. Wiles, 2 New Pots 12½
L. Todhunter, 1 scythe 1.00
I Corwin, 1 corn Riddle 06½
I. Hathaway, 1 sickle 06½
I. Drake, 1 pr stirups 18¼
N. Scott, 1 pr pincers 06½
F. Lucas, 1 box and contents of old iron 1.00
N. Scott, Rasp 18½
Wm. Kirby, 1 breast and halter chain 31½
R. Little, 1 5ft chain 3.00
I. Brandenburg, 1 foot adz 31
Z. Stubbs, 1 coopers adz 62½
E. Lefevre, 1 cow chain 25
E. Share, 3 augurs 62½
Mrs. Share, 2 cow chains 75
E. Share, 2 coffee roasters 12½
E. Stowell, 1 wagon jack—old 1.00
E. Share, 2 flour barrels 12½
Mrs. Share, 1 Bridle 50
E. Lefevre, 1 man's saddle 1.18
H. Harner, 1 set of boiler 3.50
B. Kesling, 1 set of scantling 1.37½
Mrs. Share, 6 posts 31
Jos Brandenburg, 1 Wagon and bed 33.13½
          8 per cent discount for prompt payment
E. Robinson, 1 set of harness 14.25
R. Little, fly straps 3.00
I. Corwin, Hay bed 12½
B. Hathaway, 1 little spotted cow 4.50
C. H. Abby, 1 large white cow 13.00
I. Corwin, 1 black bull 3.75
E. Stowell, 1 red heifer 5.31
E. Share, 1 white steer 5.50
H. Miller, set of boards in stable yard 62½
Wm. M. Wiles, American Speeches . . . .

do	1 halter chain	
Jos. Edwards, Bryce scythe		
A. Wright, lot of iron		
G. Rankin, And Irons		
Dr. Van Harlingen, shovel and tongs		
Jos. Foote, 3 chairs		
A. Osborn, 1 doz old chairs		2.62
Wm. M. Wiles, 1 chest		.81
E. LeFevre, 1 circular bureau		6.50
G. Rankins, 44 bu wheat		18.00
E. Share, wodden shovel		.31
H. Miller, 4 boxes		.40
J. Foote, 2 boxes		.31
J. Frasier, large steel yards		2.00
G. Rankins, 4 empty barrels		.18
I. Todhunter, 1 keg with timothy seed		.18
Wm. M. Wiles, 1 box and contents		.81
Mrs. Share, barrel with hoops, and keg of soap		.25
do	1 set quilting frames	.43
do	2 barrels	.37½
Wm. Pence, 1 wire riddle		.37
Jas Frasier, 1 seive		.25
Wm. P. Thatcher, 2 baggs		.50
E. Share, 2 baggs		.25
Mrs. Share, 1 old table and two old benches		
S. Locke, 1 tub		.12
Mrs. Share, 1 clothes dryer		.56
L. Todhunter, 1 rope		.43
I. Conery, 2 funnels and gal. measure		.18
Wm. Manning, 1 cash with gin 5 gals.		2.12½
I. Conery, ¼ doz beer bottles		.52
do	do	.54
do	do	.38
Jas Frasier	do	.37
do	do	.25
A. Wright, 2 barrels of vinegar		3.18
Mrs. Share, 2 do		4.37
Henry Howe, 1		1.75
R. Little, 1		1.62
A. F. Neal, ½barrel of cordial		3.80
Wm. Alloway, 1 do		1.80
do	1 cask currant wine	2.12
Wm. M. Wiles, 1 keg and contents		.87

L. Connery, 1 Barrel gin		2.78
Henry Miller, 1 empty barrel		.12
E. LeFevre, 1 corn harrow		3.00
E. Share, 1 plow		4.50
T. Bretney, 1 large harrow		3.37
T. Smith, 1 pr double trees		1.31
Robert Porter, 1 old plow		1.62½
Thomas Smith, Carriage		167.50
do Carriage Harness		16.75
James Liddle, 1 blind horse		26.00
Rich'd Little, 1 large bay horse		75.00
I. Van Horn, 1 small bay colt		11.00
E. Share, 1 roan colt		26.00
Wm. Alloways, 6 hogs		14.00
R. Little, 13 pigs		7.25
Mrs. Share, 8 shoats		7.00
do 8 fat hogs		20.00
Thomas Smith, Lines and collar		.50
James Bone, Lease on 30 acres Sect. 29 R 33		223.00
		$813.00

A true list signed by
A. H. Dunlavy
Thos Corwin

List of Distinguished Guests

FOR WHOM ROOMS HAVE BEEN NAMED

Wm. Howard Taft, 1857-1930. 27th President. Born in Ohio. Chief Justice U. S. Supreme Court.

Robert A. Taft, 1889-1953. U. S. Senate. Best known as "Mr. Republican."

Warren G. Harding, 1865-1923. 29th President. Born in Ohio. Harding's campaign slogan "Back to normalcy" won his election with Calvin Coolidge as Vice President.

William McKinley, 1843-1901. 25th President. Born in Ohio. American Statesman, Governor of Ohio.

James A. Garfield, 1831-1881. 20th President. Born in Ohio. Was last U. S. President born in a log cabin.

Cordell Hull, 1871-1955. As Secretary of State he contributed to our "Good Neighbor Policy" toward Latin America. Educated at the National Normal University.

U. S. Grant, 1822-1885. 18th President. Born in Ohio. West Point Graduate. General in Civil War.

Henry Clay, 1777-1852. American Statesman.
Kentucky's most noted orator. Frequent visitor on way to Washington or to Lexington, Kentucky.

Clement Vallandigham, 1820-1871. Lawyer and Politician.
Exiled during the Civil War for leadership of Peace Democrats or "Copperheads." As counsel for defense he shot himself accidentally while demonstrating a move he planned to make in court.

Charles Dickens, 1812-1870. English novelist.
Stopped here on his American Tour April 20, 1842.

Wm. Henry Harrison, 1773-1841. 9th President.
Frequent Visitor.

Benjamin Harrison, 1833-1901. 23rd President. Born in Ohio.
Campaigned here 1883.

Martin Van Buren, 1782-1862. 8th President.
His proposal to establish an independent treasury became a cardinal principle of American Finance.

Rutherford B. Hayes, 1822-1893. 19th President. Born in Ohio.
Governor of Ohio 1868-1872 and 1876-1877.

John McLean, 1785-1861. Founder of *The Western Star,* Feb. 13, 1807. Printed first Shaker Book. Member of Congress. Judge Ohio Supreme Court. Commissioner U. S. Land Office. Postmaster General. U. S. Supreme Court.

John Quincy Adams, 1767-1848. 6th President.
Visited here when he came west to dedicate *The Cincinnati Observatory* for Ormsby Mitchel, Nov. 5th, 1843. He sat for two portraits by Marcus Mote.

Thomas Corwin, 1794-1865. Ohio Representative. U. S. Congress. Governor of Ohio. U. S. Senate. Secretary of Treasury. U. S. Minister to Mexico.

Edwin Forrest, 1806-1872. Shakespearean Actor.
Was here three weeks in 1823 with a troupe of players believed to be first theatrical company in Lebanon.

Ormsby Mitchel, 1809-1862. Lived in Lebanon. Attended West Point.
Was Civil War General. Founded *Cincinnati Observatory.*

"The Spy Glass out on the hill
Is now entirely finished.
The distance twixt us and the moon
Is sensibly diminished.

When Mitchel looks, it comes near
He sees the hills and trees
Which most conclusively doth prove
That 'tis not made of cheese."
      —*Cincinnati Enquirer,* 1845

De Witt Clinton, 1769-1828. Statesman—Philanthropist.
Govenor of New York. Was here in 1825 to inaugurate Ohio's
canal system.   *
Alfred Holbrook, 1819-1909. Teacher of Teachers.
Founded National Normal University 1855. To him is credited
vitalized recitation, short-term unit and year 'round system of
college.
Ethan Allen Brown, 1776-1852. Governor of Ohio 1818-1822.
Member of Canal Commission.
Robert G. Ingersoll, 1823-1899. American lawyer, lecturer, author.
His lectures on Theology formed the basis of extensive con-
troversies. He lectured here and paid high tribute to Thomas
Corwin.
Henry Howe, 1816-1893. Ohio's Historian. Visiting here in 1846 he said:
"Ohio, the bright young state, dedicated to freedom, lay before
me a mine of rich ungarnered history."
Jeremiah Morrow, 1771-1852. Member Territorial legislature.
Ohio's First Representative. U. S. Senator. State Commissioner
of Canals. Governor of Ohio 1822-28. President of The Little
Miami Railroad.
Charles R. Sherman, 1788-1829. Judge of Ohio Supreme Court.
Father of General Wm. Tecumseh Sherman died here.
Francis Dunlavy, 1761-1839. Served in 8 Indian campaigns. Was first
teacher in Warren County. Member Territorial Legislature.
Helped frame first Ohio Constitution. President Judge 1803-1817.
James Whitcomb Riley, 1853-1916. "The Hoosier Poet."
His genius enshrined him in the heart of the nation. His best
loved poems are "Old Swimmin' Hole and "An Old Sweetheart
of Mine."
William E. Harmon, 1862-1928. Noted Philanthropist.
Established Harmon Park and Harmon Hall for Recreation and
Mollie Harmon Home for aged Gentlefolk.
Earl Derby. Then Lord Stanley, later Prime Minister of England,
with Lord Denman and Lord Dennison, all members of House of
Lords, visited for one week in 1827. They went hunting. Met and
visited with Jacob Grigg, an English teacher here.
James G. Blaine, 1830-1893. American Statesman. Orator and Party
organizer. Campaigned for President here.
Harriet Beecher Stowe, 1811-1896. Author of "Uncle Tom's Cabin."
With sister Catherine tried to establish school here.
Henry Ward Beecher, 1813-1887. American Clergyman. Antislavery
lecturer, Temperance leader.

Edward D. Mansfield, 1801-1880. Teacher, Author and Editor. Married Margaret Worthington, daughter of Governor Thomas Worthington.

Wendell Phillips, 1811-1884. Abolitionist Leader. Lectured here.

August Belmont, 1816-1890. Great Financier of The Empire State. Visited here in 1883 and attended the Warren County Fair.

James Fennesy. The last Shaker from Union Village. Moved here with his own furniture when Union Village was sold to the United Brethren Church.

William Henry Venable, 1836-1920. Teacher and Author. Attended N.N.U. Best known for "Beginnings of Literary Culture in the Ohio Valley." Textbooks and poems.

Horace Mann, 1796-1859. American Educator and Author. Member of Congress. President of Antioch College 1852-1859.

Joseph Benson Foraker, 1846-1917. Governor of Ohio 1886-1890. U. S. Senator.

Marcus Mote, 1817-1898. Pioneer Quaker Artist.

Samuel L. Clemens, 1835-1910. "Mark Twain." Immortalized Tom Sawyer and Huckelberry Finn.

William Dean Howells, 1837-1920. Author and Critic. Newspaperman in Hamilton, Dayton and Columbus. Visited frequently.

Elbert G. Hubbard, 1856-1915. American writer, editor and printer. Established The Roycroft Shop which developed the colony of artists and artisans known as Roycrofters. He wrote of Thomas Corwin in his "Little Journeys to the homes of great men."

Morris Birkbeck, 1764-1825. English Traveler and Author. Visited in 1817.

The list is far from complete. Guests were chosen because of their popular appeal. No living guest has been included in the present list.

Taverns in Warren County

Taverns in this area, prior to 1803, were licensed in Hamilton County. Several are known to have been here, including Ephraim Hathaway's "Black Horse" in Lebanon, David Sutton's in Deerfield and Joseph Crane's in Franklin.

The original license issued to Crane on May 5, 1801 is the only one we have been able to locate.

In four years thirty taverns were licensed to operate in Warren County. There were six taverns in Lebanon in July 1839.

The following list of taverns and tavern keepers has been compiled from court documents, advertisements in *The Western Star* and other papers, Beer's History of Warren County, Census Records, Josiah Morrow's writings and from family histories.

Some of these old taverns had very interesting names. A few are listed here:

The Black Horse	The Ohio and Pennsylvania Hotel
The Golden Lamb	Washington Hall
The Red Lion	The George Washington
The Blue Ball	Sign of George Washington
The Black Bear	on Horseback
The Spread Eagle	The Indian Chief
The White Horse	The Indian Queen
Two White Horses	The Goddess of Liberty
The Lion and Eagle	Liberty House
The Bull's Head	Clinton Hotel
The Red Buck	Henry Clay House
The Black Hawk	Sign of General Jackson
The Green Tree	General Jackson on Horseback
Cross Keys	White Hall
Sign of the Crossed Keys	The National Hotel

List of Early Taverns and Keepers

Abbey, C. H. . . . . Ohio Coffee House, 1831
Armstrong, Walter 1810
Armstrong, Mr. . . . . 1813 Cross Road, 6 miles east of Lebanon
Bacon, Joseph . . . . 1808 Lebanon
Baen, Joseph 1809
Baird, Samuel . . . . Before 1818 at The Green Tree
Baird, John . . . . After 1818 at The Green Tree
Boal, Robert (came from Pennsylvania) The Red Buck, 8 miles west
  of Lebanon
Ball, Calvin 1806-1808
Ball, Christiana 1809-1810
Baker, David . . . . On S. W. Cor. Broadway and Mulberry,
  later on Mulberry
Baldwin, Francis . . . . 1806 Lebanon
Billmire House (later Lyceum) N. W. Cor. Silver and East
Birdsall, James 1808-1810
Black Bear . . . . North of Waynesville
Black Hawk . . . . East of Lebanon
Bradley, Calvin . . . . 1804-1805, and 1839 and later at The
  Golden Lamb and The Bradley House
Brady, William 1807

56

Buckman's Tavern . . . . 1822 Lebanon

Burch House . . . . W. M. Burch, Mason 1825

Bull's Head . . . . Cor. Mulberry and Mechanic. Bell in belfry rang about midnight December 23, 1832 when Abner Ross was born. He became a tavern keeper.

Crane's Tavern . . . . 1801 Franklin

Crane, Jonathan . . . . 1820 The Red Lion

Chalburn, Fiory 1809

Conery, James D. . . . . The Spread Eagle South of Lebanon

Carty, Benjamin 1806-1808

Coleman, Washington (Born New Jersey 1811) Franklin

Corwin, Ichabod . . . . Black Horse 1798 or 99 Lebanon The Green Tree (builder of both)

Clinton, Samuel . . . . 1806 Waynesville

Cunningham, Richard . . . . . 1806-1809 Lebanon

Clay House . . . . Wm. M. Wiles, Wm. Wiles and E. A. Wiles, Lebanon

Cushing, Daniel 1809-1810

Cloud, Abner 1806

Conery, Jonathan . . . . 1806-1808 Lebanon

Corbly, William K. . . . . 1845 White Hall - near Court House formerly owned by Jabish Phillips

Dearth, Edward . . . . 1803-1807-1809 Franklin

Dill, Joseph 1804-1806

Dickerson, Walter . . . . . . 1806-1808-1810 Deerfield Twp.

Eagle Tavern . . . . 1829 opposite corner to The Red Lion

Earhart, Martin Jr. . . . . 1808-1809-1810 Franklin

Earhart and Finney . . . . 1826 Franklin

Enoch, Isaac 1806

Egbert, David . . . . 1843 Exchange Hotel Lebanon

Egbert, Samuel . . . . 1845 Mansion House on Main St., Lebanon. Also Williamson House 1848

Finney . . . . 1826 Franklin

Ferguson, William . . . . . . 1805-7-8-9-10 Lebanon 1823-1829 The Indian Chief

Foster, Daniel . . . . 1809 At Foster's Crossing

Fisher, Daniel 1809

Goodwin, Thomas . . . . 1803 At Waynesville

Goodwin, Wm. M. . . . . 1806-1808 Waynesville

Gustin, Benajah . . . . 1849 At Red Lion

Hathaway, Ephraim . . . . . 1801-3-4. etc. Black Horse and later at The Golden Lamb

Harrison, Wm. Henry . . . . . 1825 Main Street, Franklin
Heaton, Samuel 1810
Hall, John . . . . The Red Buck, W. of Lebanon (not Red Lion)
Hildreth, Joseph . . . . Eagle Tavern, at Red Lion
Hill, James . . . . 1816 Broadway, Lebanon
Hill, A. . . . . 1815 The Golden Lamb
Hollingsworth, Joshua . . . . . 1809 The Spread Eagle
Hunt, Aaron 1806-7-8-10
Halsey, Christopher . . . . 1806 Near Waynesville
Hutchinson, Mr. . . . . 1822 Kept Buckman's Tavern
Jameson, Samuel . . . . The Indian Queen, Cincinnati Road
Jennings, James . . . . 1806-1807 Waynesville
Jorden, John 1810
Kelsey, John . . . . 1833 Washington Hall, Springboro
Kiphart, John . . . . 1821 Clarksville
Kibby, Joseph . . . . 1803 Deerfield
Leonard, ... 1817 General Jackson on Horseback
                                   Lebanon
Lowry, Wm. . . . . 1834 Washington Hotel
Mickle, W. S. . . . . 1836 Goddess of Liberty, Roachester
Moorhouse, James . . . . 1808 Lebanon
McCain, Robert 1806-1807
McCarty, ... 5 miles north of Lebanon on Dayton Pike
McCashen, John . . . . 1803-6-9 Franklin
McCashen, Robert . . . . 1808-1810 Franklin
Munger, Col. H. . . . . 1830 Henry Clay House in Lebanon
Neal, Alonzo F. . . . .
Noble, William . . . . 1806 Lebanon
Obergefel, M. . . . . Liberty House Foster's Crossing
O'Dell, Chris . . . . 1823 Traveler's Rest North of Lebanon on
                                   Dayton Pike
Parshall, Richard . . . . 1816 Sign of George Washington Lebanon
                                   Sign of General Jackson
                                   General Jackson on Horseback
Patton, William . . . . 1825 Ridgeville
Phares, Robert 1809-1810
Phillips, Jabish . . . . Before 1845 White Hall Tavern Lebanon
Phillips, Major . . . . 1821 Sign of the Crossed Keys Lebanon
                                   2 story brick West side of Broadway
                                   between Main and Mulberry
Probasco, Peter 1834
Reeder, Elijah . . . . 1803-6-8 Lebanon
Reeder, Daniel . . . . 1807-1821 Lebanon

Reeder, Stephen 1810
Roe, Daniel . . . . 1806 Lebanon
Rue, Benjamin . . . . The Crossed Keys Fort Ancient
                        The Golden Lamb
                        The Indian Chief
Ream, Benjamin . . . . 1837 Ream's Hotel (formerly Henry Clay
                        House)
Sanders, John . . . . 1819 Tavern and Toll Gate Fosters
Seaman, Jonas . . . . 1803 The Golden Lamb Lebanon
Share, Henry . . . . 1820-1830 The Golden Lamb Lebanon
Share, Mary . . . . 1830-1837 The Golden Lamb Lebanon
Share, Ephraim . . . . Franklin
Silver, Seth . . . . 1809 Waynesville
Sinnard, William . . . . 1816 Bought George Washington from
                        R. Parshall
Smith, Thomas . . . . 1826 Lebanon
Snider, Conrod . . . . 1809 Lebanon
South, Thomas . . . . 1824 Mulberry Street, Lebanon
Sharp, Nathan . . . . The Green Tree (formerly a Shaker at
                        Union Village)
Stansel, Jere . . . . 1837 Washington Hall Springboro
Stubbs, Isaac . . . . 1841 and later, in 1843 The Golden Lamb
Stubbs, Albert and others . The Golden Lamb Lebanon
Spencer, John . . . . 1808 to 1820 The Crossed Keys Lebanon
                        later sold to Major Phillips and others
Squires, Elias . . . . 1803 Franklin Twp.
Sutton, David . . . . 1805 etc. Deerfield
Thomas, Elijah . . . . 1826 Sign of Lion and Eagle, Roachester
Traveler's Rest . . . . 1823 Three miles North of Lebanon
Tuttle, P. E. . . . . 1845 Williamson House Lebanon
                        Formerly of Tuttle House Piqua
Upton, Mathew . . . . 1818 The Green Tree Franklin
Woods, Emy . . . . 1803 Franklin
Woodward, Levi 1806
Worrell, John . . . . 1816 Union Hotel Waynesville
Wiles, William M (oon) . . . . 1826 National Hotel Lebanon
                        Lately of The Henry Clay House
Wiles, William . . . . Henry Clay House Lebanon
Wiles, E. A. . . . . 1854 Henry Clay on Broadway, S. W. of
                        old Court House
Williamson, G. P. . . . . 1843 Williamson House, S. E. Cor.
                        Silver and Broadway, Lebanon
White Horse . . . . 1812 West Main St. Lebanon
Washington Hall . . . . Springboro